Mommy, What is Celiac Disease?

Text and illustrations copyright © 2010 by Katie Chalmers.

Mommy, What is Celiac Disease?
Awareness Press, LLC
ISBN#: 978-0-9828711-0-2

Background photos on cover and
pgs. 1, 2, 5, 9, 20, 24, 26, 28: ©iStockphoto.com.

"Honey, while we're at the park today,
I want to talk to you about something…"

"Okay, Mommy…about what?"

"Well, do you remember all those tests your doctor had you take? He called to let us know that you have something called Celiac disease."

"Mommy, what is Celiac disease? Does it mean I'm too silly?"

"No, silly, having Celiac disease means that there are some things you can't eat anymore. But the good news is that there are still many wonderful things you CAN eat!"

"That's good Mommy...so can I still eat potato chips and popcorn... and corn chips?"

"Yes, you can still eat those tasty snacks."

"Well, can I still eat all my favorite fruits, like grapes, apples and Poppa's raspberries? Will we still pick strawberries and blueberries in the summertime?"

"Yes...you can eat any fruit you like. Plus, you can also eat all your favorite veggies, too, like fresh peas from the pod, carrots, tomatoes and corn."

"Oh, good. What about
Lindsey's birthday party?
Can I have cake and ice cream?"

"You'll get to bring a special cupcake
or something to the party, to have
instead of the cake, but you can
probably eat the ice cream."

"Oh, goodie.
I like ice cream better anyhow…
What about candy?"

"Sweetie, you'll be happy to hear that
there are *many, many* kinds of candy
you can still eat!"

"Phew... Well, can I still
eat chicken tenders?
And meatballs?
Hamburgers and hotdogs?
What about all my favorite
sandwiches?"

"Yep. We just need to make the
chicken and meatballs a special
way, and you'll eat special rolls
and sandwich bread. The reason
I call those things 'special' is
because they are made without
something called gluten."

"Mommy, what is gluten?"

"That's a very good question. Most people don't know what gluten is, but it's in lots of foods, like bread, crackers, pasta, cereal, soup and all sorts of food. Our new job is to make sure that you don't eat anything with gluten in it. Our whole family will help you to learn how to do it yourself someday. Won't that be fun?"

"Yes, Mommy, that will be fun, *but, Mommy*...

...What IS gluten?!"

"Well, gluten is inside certain grains like wheat, barley and rye. So we need to read food labels and make sure you don't eat anything made from those grains. We'll learn all about it... together."

"But mommy, *why* can't I have gluten anymore?"

"Because, when you are a Celiac, your body gets hurt inside whenever you eat gluten...

...Some kids with Celiac disease don't feel anything when they eat it, but other kids can always tell when they eat gluten — they'll get a bad tummy ache and need to run to the potty. Everyone handles it differently, but for *all* Celiacs, gluten is hurting their bodies even when they can't tell on the outside."

"But, Mommy, *where* inside my body does it get hurt?"

"Remember how you crawled through that tube before? Well, there's a long, curly organ inside your body, called your small intestine, which helps digest your food. It kind of looks like that pile of worms you collected! Your food goes through your intestine just like you crawled through that tube.

Inside of your small intestine are these teeny, tiny things called 'villi'. Their job is to take all the vitamins, protein, calcium and good things from food and put all of it in your body, which helps you grow big and strong…"

"But when you are a Celiac, gluten is an enemy to your body. So when you eat gluten, your body tries to protect itself by attacking and hurting your villi. It flattens them out so they don't work right — kind of like the grass we just stomped down! And the only way to get the villi working again is to make sure you don't eat any gluten."

"Once your villi are healed, you'll grow tall and be stronger and healthier. We need to make sure that you never let gluten into your body again, not even a little bit. Because gluten could cause problems in many different parts of your body someday if you keep eating it. I know we can do it because we're a great team!"

"Mommy, did I catch it
from somebody?

"Oh, no, it's just something you were
born with, honey. You didn't catch it
from anybody and no one can catch
it from you. It doesn't even have
anything to do with germs."

"Do I have to take
medicine for it?"

"Nope, no medicine. As long as you
don't eat any gluten, you'll be as
strong and healthy as all the other
kids. You'll play sports, go to new
places and have fun at parties,
just like everyone else. The only
difference is that you'll need to be
careful about what you eat."

"Actually, our whole family will be healthier than ever now! We are going to eat lots of gluten-free foods *with* you. We are going to try new, healthy, yummy recipes together, and find some special treats for you to eat. Our family loves you and will *always* help you with this...

You know, you're a lucky kid. There are tons of gluten-free foods out there. You won't *believe* all of the delicious things we are going to discover together!"

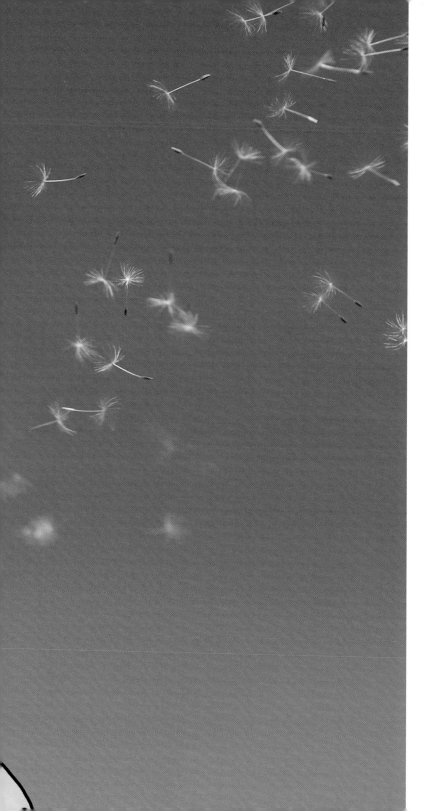

"And, don't feel like you're the only one… because guess what? There are MILLIONS of people in the world with Celiac disease, but only a tiny number of those people even know they have it. We can help by telling others about it. We can spread the word, just like you're blowing that dandelion fluff around!

You're very lucky, because your doctors figured it out early enough so your body can heal itself. Now that we know, gluten won't keep hurting you, so every day in every way you'll feel better and better!"

"So, remember to think positive and look at the sunny side of Celiac. Other than some food, everything else about your life will be just like other kids.

And anyhow, eating is such a small part of life, isn't it?
There are so many more fun things to think about..."

"Mommy, I think I'm going to be good at this…

Let's go home and find our aprons!"

To make the transition to a gluten-free diet
a bit easier for your family, may we present:

Our Family's Favorites*

Schär

Schar makes our family's favorite **pastas**. We also love their thin, crispy breadsticks and cheese bites. For quick meals we make french bread pizza & garlic bread on their parbaked sub rolls & baguettes.

NATURE'S PATH ORGANIC
EnviroKidz ORGANIC

Morgan's 2 favorite **cereals** are made by this eco-friendly company: *Honey'd Corn Flakes* and *EnviroKidz Peanut Butter Panda Puffs.* Their flavored rice bars also make great school snacks.

Pamela's PRODUCTS

Our favorite **dessert mixes** by far. We love their brownies, cupcakes and unbelievably decadent frosting, and make the best chocolate chip cookies & pie crusts with their baking mixes.

chēbē Bread. *Slightly unusual. Unusually good.*

Our favorite brand for so many things: Morgan's sandwich rolls, pizza crust, breadsticks and garlic bread. Their **mixes** are very easy to make and to work with, and we love the taste!

ORGANIC MARY'S Gone CRACKERS

For snacks we often enjoy our favorite Mary's **herb crackers** with cheese. And we dip their "sticks & twigs" into hummus & dips.

SNYDER'S OF HANOVER

We all love their great tasting, low-fat **pretzel sticks** and EatSmart Naturals tortilla chips. Both are certified G-F and made in U.S.A.

Wegmans

This store is a Godsend. They label all of their **store brands** with a G-F logo and have a large G-F section in their Nature's Marketplace. Find their G-F product list online, plus cooking videos & more.

*Note to parents: G-F means gluten-free. These *really* are our family's favorite brands, after much trial and error, yet please note that this is not a guarantee that you will love them as much as we do. Hopefully this will save you time and money as you transition your child into his or her new gluten-free diet. See website for more information on these and other products by these brands. Good luck and stay positive!

Learn much more at:
www.katiechalmers.com

- positive parenting articles & insights
- links to National Celiac Foundations and Celiac Research Centers
- links to helpful G-F websites
- favorite food products information
- favorite G-F recipes & diet tips
- resources for family, friends & school